A true story from the Bible

Jesus was coming to dinner!

And Martha was
busy, busy, busy ...

"Just a minute!"

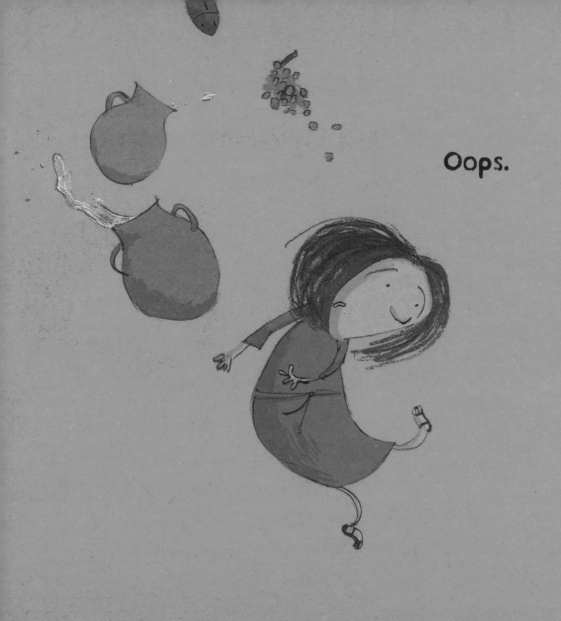

Oops.

Splat!

But Mary ...
where was Mary?

Not in the kitchen.

Not in the hall.

Mary was not busy at all!

There she is, just sitting down still
- listening to Jesus!

"Not helping one bit!"
said Martha.

"Hmmmmphhhh!"

"Tell her to help!"
Martha said.

But Jesus didn't do that.

He said, "Martha, Martha,
you're all in a flap!"

"But there's only one thing
                      that really matters."

"You just need to listen to me, like Mary."

And we can listen to Jesus too.

Because listening to him
is the best thing to do!

Notes for grown-ups

This story comes from Luke 10 v 38-42. Mary and Martha, and their brother Lazarus, were all friends of Jesus. When Jesus came to visit their home, the two women acted very differently. Mary sat at Jesus's feet listening to him, but Martha was rushing around getting everything ready for their guest.

When Martha saw that Mary wasn't helping, she complained to Jesus, *"Lord, don't you care that my sister has left me to do the work by myself? Tell her to help me!"* (v 40, NIV)

But Jesus told her that Mary had made the best choice: *"Martha, Martha,"* the Lord answered, *"you are worried and upset about many things, but few things are needed—or indeed only one. Mary has chosen what is better, and it will not be taken away from her"* (v 41-42, NIV).

Listening to Jesus is always the best thing to do!

Luke 10 v 38-42

(The Bible: New International Version)

38 As Jesus and his disciples were on their way, he came to a village where a woman named Martha opened her home to him. 39 She had a sister called Mary, who sat at the Lord's feet listening to what he said. 40 But Martha was distracted by all the preparations that had to be made. She came to him and asked, "Lord, don't you care that my sister has left me to do the work by myself? Tell her to help me!"

41 "Martha, Martha," the Lord answered, "you are worried and upset about many things, 42 but few things are needed—or indeed only one. Mary has chosen what is better, and it will not be taken away from her."

⋛Little me⋚
BIG GOD

Collect the series:

• The Man Who Would Not Be Quiet   • Never Too Little
• The Best Thing To Do

For Micah.
Praying you'll listen to God first,
no matter what others say, as Mary did.
S. W.

The best thing to do
© Stephanie Williams, 2019

Published by:
The Good Book Company

thegoodbook.com | www.thegoodbook.co.uk
thegoodbook.com.au | thegoodbook.co.nz | thegoodbook.co.in

ISBN: 9781784983840 | Printed in India